WOODSTOCK

3 DAYS of PEACE & MUSIC

First published in 2019
by Murray Books (Australia)
www.murraybooks.com

Copyright © 2019 Murray Books (Australia)
Copyright © 2015 Peter Murray
Licensed to G2 Entertainment UK

ISBN 978-1-78281-488-7

Compiled by Peter Murray and Lorri Lynn

Images: Shutterstock, Public Domain

The author and publisher have made every effort to ensure the information contained in this book was
correct at the time of going to press and accept no responsibility for any loss, injury or inconvenience
sustained by any person or organisation using this book. Some editorial and imagery may have been used
from the Public Domain.

CONTENTS

THE PLAN

Woodstock began as a plan by Artie Kornfield and Michael Lang to finance the design and construction of a small recording studio in Woodstock, New York. The pair wanted to build a studio in a rural, wooded setting, and they approached entrepreneurs John P. Roberts and Joel Rosenman in 1969 as a means of securing the finance they needed. Roberts and Rosenman were in the process of building the large New York based Media Sound Studio, and while the 'studio-in-the-woods' concept did not appeal to them, the idea of organising a concert in the Woodstock area did. At the time, Woodstock was frequented by artists such as The Band, Bob Dylan and others, and Lang's success with the Miami Pop Festival in 1968 provided the experience needed to stage a large event. Roberts and Rosenman agreed to finance the festival, and the four music promoters formed Woodstock Ventures in January, 1969.

Woodstock Ventures began life as a profit-making venture, and no expense was spared in transforming its Manhattan offices into a psychedelic wonderland for all who visited. While Lang and Kornfield set about finding a suitable venue, Roberts and Rosenman worked hard to sign a big-name group as a means of attracting other big names. It took three months before Woodstock Ventures had its first signed contract, and the group that accepted $10,000 to play for 50 minutes was the hugely popular Creedence Clearwater Revival. With the ink barely dry on the contract, other big-names jumped on board for the August festival advertised as "three days of peace and love".

Lang and Kornfield had a more relaxed method of conducting business than Roberts and Rosenman, and following confusion over securing the venue and concern over the amount of money already spent, the latter took over the search. The pair found a 300 acre industrial park in the town of Wallkill and took out a lease for $10,000. As part of the deal, no more than 50,000 people were allowed to attend, but the local population were horrified at the thought of up to 50,000 hippies descending upon them. Under pressure, the Wallkill Town Board then passed a new law that required a permit for any gathering involving more than 5,000 people, and then banned the proposed concert on the grounds of portable toilets failing to meet town codes. While the festival suddenly had no home, it nevertheless gained a lot of publicity as a result of the ban. When an alternative venue was found 45 miles away at the farm of dairy farmer Max Yasgur, it

was the Bethel Town Board that was told that there would be no more than 50,000 people attending. It was also the Bethel Town Board that refused to issue formal permits for the festival to go ahead, in spite of work beginning on Yasgur's farm following approval by the town's attorney and its building inspector.

At that point, a stop-work order was issued, leaving the organisers facing ruin in the face of local protests that included placard waving and threats to veto the purchase of milk from the Yasgur's dairy farm. Again, the publicity was a bonus for the festival's organisers, but the acts were booked, time was running out and over 186,000 advance tickets had been sold through New York City record stores and the Radio City Post Office in Manhattan. The cost of tickets was $18, and those who wanted to pay on arrival were to be charged $24.

The late change to the venue from Wallkill to Bethel had already placed construction crews under pressure, and the stop work order compounded the situation. Suddenly, the promoters had to decide between completing the fence and ticket booths or completing the stage (which was a turntable affair), as there was neither the time nor the money to do both once the stop work order was lifted. Three days prior to the August 15 event, it was the audience that made the decision when they began arriving early in their tens of thousands and simply walked onto Yasgur's farm - many without tickets. Suddenly, the Woodstock Music & Art Fair became a free festival, and "three days of peace and music" were enjoyed by more than 400,000 people.

Roberts, Rosenman, Lang and Kornfield were very nearly bankrupted by the unstoppable transformation of Woodstock into a free festival, but they were saved by the recording and film rights that had also been part of their plan. In 1970, the hit documentary "Woodstock" was released to exceptional reviews. The film cost $600,000 to produce and took in $50 million at the Box Office as well as netting an Academy Award for Best Documentary Feature.

THE FESTIVAL

When the massive influx of festival-goers began arriving in Bethel, their presence resulted in an unprecedented traffic jam. Local authorities feared chaos, so no traffic codes were enforced and the build-up continued. Radio stations began announcements as far away as the Manhattan offices of Woodstock Ventures, and television stations tried to discourage people from attending in light of the New York State Thruway reportedly closing. Naturally, very few festival-goers heeded the voice of authority and the crowds continued to build along roads and through fields that had become muddy in light of recent rains. Never before had the roads of New York State been so filled with colour, sound and a sense of peaceful purpose than they did in August, 1969, packed with all manner of bohemian people and vehicles intent upon sharing their love of music and peace to the sounds of 32 performers over four days.

More than 400,000 people were too much for the provided facilities, with food and sanitation in short supply, but the atmosphere was a peaceful one regardless of the privations. The bad weather continued in bursts, but when it was fine, skinny dipping in Fillippini Pond became the order of the day behind the stage at the bottom of Max Yasgur's property. Every square inch of the dairy farmer's land was filled with the sights, smells and sounds of a generation committed to peace, love and harmony, and the only fatalities were an accident involving a tractor and a death from insulin usage. At least two babies were born during Woodstock, but no statistics exist to support the number of conceptions.

As the Governor of New York considered calling out the National Guard, and while Sullivan County declared a State of Emergency, the US Air Force provided air transport for the festival's performers. The stage had been completed in time (at the cost of fencing and ticket booths) and sound had been specifically engineered to suit the "sound bowl" conditions on Yasgur's farm. Speaker columns of 70 feet high sat on hills around the area, each sporting 16 loudspeaker arrangements in a square and known as "Woodstock Bins". Power was supplied by three transformers. By 5:00pm on Friday, August 15 1969, Woodstock was ready to begin. By 8:30 am on Monday morning when Jimi Hendrix took the stage as the final act, the world of music would have its most defining moment in living memory, and an entire generation would remember Woodstock for the ensuing half century.

CHIP MONCK - THE EMCEE

When Monck was hired by the promoters of Woodstock Ventures, it was to build the staging and lighting for the Woodstock Festival in its original location at Wallkill, New York. When permission was withdrawn for the festival to go ahead at Wallkill, Monck and his crew were forced to re-think much of their original design.

Once Yasgur's Farm was secured at Bethel, Monck had to deal with a seriously shortened construction schedule. As a result, the hastily completed stage roof was not strong enough to support the rented lighting, so most of the lighting remained unused and sat under the stage floor. The result was a poorly flood-lit stage that was difficult to film.

Just before the concert began on the Friday, promoter Michael Lang realised that he had forgotten to hire a Master of Ceremonies, so he drafted Chip Monck to fill the role. No stranger to the world of staging and lighting, Monck was nevertheless thrust into the emcee spotlight in front of the music world's largest ever audience.

Until Woodstock, Monck had worked behind the scenes of most of America's largest music festivals, and credits included The Village Gate in the early 1960s when Peter, Paul and Mary were huge, Harlem's Apollo and Dylan's first electric concert in Newport. In Altamont, Monck had lost teeth when struck by a rug-stealing Hell's Angel wielding a pool cue, but he felt strongly enough about the stage carpet he had designed to hang onto it.

After Woodstock, Monck was instrumental in tours by The Rolling Stones, and Peter Gabriel, as well as the infamous Rumble in the Jungle between Mohammed Ali and George Foreman and the heady days of Vegas and its incredible stage shows.

Of his sudden promotion to Emcee at Woodstock, Monck says, "*I was petrified, but I got to the point where I was practically paternal in some periods of dire emergency.*" His most notable announcements during the festival came about as a result of people climbing on the towers and the state of the LSD circulating at the venue. For the tower climbers, he recalls announcing, "*Get the f**k down; do you know what you're doing?*" and to those concerned about the quality of drugs, he made the following announcement:

"*To get back to the warning that I've received, you might take it with however many grains of salt you wish, that the brown acid that is circulating around us is not specifically too good. It's suggested that you do stay away from that. Of course, it's your own trip, so be my guest but please be advised that there's a warning on that one; okay?*"

Not one person died of a drug overdose at Woodstock.

THE LINEUP

Friday Night to Saturday Morning

Richie Havens

Swami Satchidananda

Sweetwater

Bert Sommer

Tim Hardin

Ravi Shankar

Melanie Safka

Arlo Guthrie

Joan Baez

On Stage
5:07pm – 7:00pm
Playlist
From the Prison
Get Together
From the Prison (reprise)
The Minstrel from Gault
I'm a Stranger Here
High Flying Bird
I Can't Make It Anymore
With a Little Help from My Friends
Handsome Johnny
Strawberry Fields Forever / Hey Jude
Freedom (Motherless Child)

Singer-songwriter and guitarist Richie Havens was well known for his covers of folk and pop songs and his unique and intense style of rhythm guitar. As the opening act, he was asked to extend his performance time to cover those acts who were stuck in standstill traffic jams. He was accompanied by Daniel Ben Zebulon on percussion and Paul "Deano" Williams on guitar and backing vocals. Havens performed a number of encores and had exhausted his own repertoire when he was again asked for more. Suddenly inspired, he played an improvised song based on "Motherless Child", an old spiritual that became "Freedom" and helped Havens to reach a worldwide audience through the release of the 1970 movie.

Full Name	Richard Pierce Havens
Known As	Richie Havens
Instruments	Vox, Sitar, Guitar
Born	January 21, 1941 Brooklyn, New York, USA
Died	April 22, 2013 Jersey City, New Jersey, USA
Age at Death	72
Genre/Style	Folk rock, blues, soul, funk

SWAMI SATCHIDANANDA

On Stage
7:10pm – 7:20pm

Playlist
Festival Invocation

Born C.K. Ranaswamy Gounder in 1914, the Indian religious teacher, yoga adept and spiritual master known as Swami Satchidananda had been an American citizen for a few years before he was called in as Woodstock's opening speaker. The author of spiritual and philosophical books had a core following in both India and the West, and he had spent many years promoting ecumenism, yoga, enlightenment and selfless service in the modern world. Following the invocation at Woodstock, Swami Satchidananda gave countless lectures and wrote many books before founding the Integral Yoga Institute. He was also the spiritual guru to many Hollywood stars and famous musicians, and opened the Light of Truth Universal Shrine (LOTUS) in Virginia in 1986.

Full Name	C.K. Ranaswamy Gounder
Known As	Swami Satchidananda
Role	Spiritual leader
Born	22 December, 1914 Chettipalayam, Coimbatore, Tamil Nadu, British India
Died	19 August, 2002 Chennai, Tamil Nadu, India
Age at Death	87

SWEETWATER

On Stage
7:30pm – 8:10pm

Playlist

Motherless Child
Look Out
For Pete's Sake
What's Wrong
Crystal Spider

Two Worlds
Why Oh Why
Let the Sunshine In
Oh Happy Day

American rock band Sweetwater were originally scheduled as Woodstock's opening act, but they were stopped by police and delayed as they headed for the festival - leaving Richie Havens to cover for them. The Los Angeles based band eventually arrived to become the first band to perform at the festival, chosen for their popularity as an opening act for The Doors, Eric Burdon and the Animals and others. Their style was a blend of psychedelic rock/fusion that would later characterise groups such as Jefferson Airplane, and their most famous recording was a version of "Motherless Child". For their Woodstock performance, the band consisted of eight performers, led by Nansi Nevins' vocals and distinctively backed by instruments that included a cello and conga drums. Less than four months after their Woodstock appearance, the band's career was cut short when Nevins was injured and brain damaged as the result of a car accident.

Band Members	Nancy "Nansi" Nevins - Lead vox/guitar August Burns - Cello (Died 1979) Albert Moore - Flute/Backing vox (Died 1994) Alan Malarowitz - Drums (Died 1981) Elpidio Cobian - Conga drums Alex Del Zoppo - Keybords Fred Herrera - Bass
Formed	Early 1960s
Genre/Style	Rock, Psychedelic rock/fusion

BERT SOMMER

On Stage
8:20pm – 9:15pm

Playlist
Jennifer
The Road to Travel
I Wondered Where You Be
She's Gone
Things Are Going My Way
And When It's Over
Jeanette
America
A Note That Read
Smile

Folk singer and songwriter Bert Sommer had previously found fame with The Left Banke in 1967 with the single "Ivy Ivy", and he spent the 1969/70 season playing Woof in the original Hair production on Broadway. It was during his eighth song, a version of Paul Simon's "America", that the crowd became electrified and gave him a standing ovation, although it was not featured in the 1970 movie. While at Woodstock, he penned his homage to the festival, "We're all Playing in the Same Band", and it was released to chart on the Billboard Hot 100 in the following year.

Full Name	Bert William Sommer
Known As	Bert Sommer
Instruments	Vox, Guitar, Piano
Born	February 7, 1949 Albany, New York, USA
Died	July 23, 1990 Troy, New York, USA
Age at Death	41
Genre/Style	Folk, Rock, Baroque Pop

TIM HARDIN

On Stage
9:20pm – 9:45pm

Playlist
How Can We Hang On to a Dream?
Susan
If I Were a Carpenter
Reason to Believe
You Upset the Grace of Living When You Lie
Speak Like a Child
Snow White Lady
Blues on My Ceiling
Simple Song of Freedom
Misty Roses

Tim Hardin was most famous for writing the hit song, "If I Were a Carpenter", which was covered by numerous artists such as Johnny Cash, Robert Plant, Bobby Darin, The Four Tops and Joan Baez. His own recording career included covers of "Hoochie Coochie Man" and "House of the Rising Sun" on the Atco label in the early sixties. Heavily blues influenced, Hardin also recorded a few more commercial numbers, but did not tour due to stage fright and a heroin habit. At Woodstock, he was backed by an entire band apart from his third number (If I Were a Carpenter), but none of the numbers were included on the soundtrack or in the 1970 film. His solo number was included in the 1994 box set, "Woodstock: Three Days of Peace and Music".

Full Name	James Timothy Hardin
Known As	Tim Hardin
Instruments	Vox, Guitar, Piano
Born	December 23, 1941 Eugene, Oregon, USA
Died	December 29, 1980 Los Angeles, California, USA
Age at Death	39
Genre/Style	Folk

RAVI SHANKAR

On Stage
10:00pm – 10:35pm

Playlist
Raga Puriya-Dhanashri / Gat In Sawarital
Tabla Solo In Jhaptal
Raga Manj Kmahaj (AIap, Jor, Dhun In Kaharwa Tal)

Indian composer and musician Ravi Shankar was a world renowned sitar player who operated the Los Angeles based Kinnara School of Music. The musician had been well received by the audience at the 1967 Monterey Pop Festival, and he had performed with many of the world's greatest classical, pop and rock stars. He published his autobiography in 1968, sharing his love and philosophy of music and its place in life as a religion. His performance at Woodstock had been eagerly awaited by tens of thousands of fans, but Shankar was not enamoured by the venue or the prevalent drug use and ultimately distanced himself from the hippie culture as a result.

Full Name	Rabindra Shankar Chowdhury
Known As	Ravi Shankar
Instruments	Sitar, Vox
Born	7 April, 1920 Benares, British India
Died	11 December, 2012 San Diego, California, USA
Age at Death	92
Genre/Style	Classical Indian

Melanie Safka

On Stage
10:50pm – 11:20pm

Playlist
Close to It All
Momma Momma
Beautiful People
Animal Crackers
Mr. Tambourine Man
Tuning My Guitar
Birthday of the Sun

Melanie Safka, also known professionally as Melanie, was one of only three women to perform as a solo artist at Woodstock. The singer-songwriter first performed as a folk singer in New York's Greenwich Village before recording with Columbia and later Buddah Records. Initially finding fame and chart success in Europe, Safka's unique talents were soon recognised in her home country, and her Woodstock performance in the rain was legendary. During Safka's set, thousands of fans lit candles or matches, inspiring her to write "Lay Down (Candles in the Rain)" about the experience. In 1970, the song became the artist's first top-ten single in the USA.

Full Name	Melanie Anne Safka
Known As	Melanie Safka Melanie
Instruments	Vox, Guitar
Born	February 3, 1947 Astoria, New York, USA
Current Age (2019)	72
Genre/Style	Folk, Country, Pop

ARLO GUTHRIE

On Stage
11:55pm – 12:25am

Playlist

> Coming into Los Angeles
> Wheel of Fortune
> Walkin' Down the Line
> Story about Moses and the Brownies
> Mary Don't You Weep
> Every Hand in the Land
> Amazing Grace

The son of famed activist and folk musician Woody Guthrie, Arlo Guthrie was renowned for his anti Vietnam War stance, as well as his pro-drugs position. His most famous recording was the 1967 album, "Alice's Restaurant", which afforded Guthrie an almost cult following through college and counter-culture radio. Arlo Guthrie's work epitomised the growing lifestyle and attitude that came to characterise the hippie movement, and he had four albums to his name when he performed at Woodstock. His arrival was preceded by rain, and although part of the stage was wet, he and his backing musicians were protected from the elements. Guthrie was accompanied by Bob Arkin on bass, John Pilla on guitar and Paul Motian on drums.

Full Name	Arlo Davy Guthrie
Known As	Arlo Guthrie
Instruments	Vox, Guitar, Piano, Harmonica, Banjo, Various wind and reed instruments
Born	July 10, 1947 Coney Island, New York, USA
Current Age (2019)	71
Genre/Style	Folk, Folk Rock, Talking Blues

Joan Baez

On Stage
12:55pm – 2:00am

Playlist

Oh Happy Day

The Last Thing on My Mind

I Shall Be Released

Story about David Harris' arrest and imprisonment

No Expectations

Joe Hill

Sweet Sir Galahad

Hickory Wind

Drug Store Truck Driving Man

I Live One Day at a Time

Take Me Back to the Sweet Sunny South

Let Me Wrap You In My Warm and Tender Love

Swing Low, Sweet Chariot

We Shall Overcome

Known for her strong activism and her successful covers of Bob Dylan songs, Joan Baez was pregnant when she stepped onto the stage at Woodstock. Baez and her husband, David Harris, had spent time in prison for their parts in anti-war and protest marches and demonstrations, and Harris was still imprisoned at the time. Baez talked about his arrest and subsequent imprisonment for refusing his military draft after her third number, affording her an immediate audience of 400,000 and a wider worldwide audience through the 1970 film release. Accompanying Baez for the number, "Truck Store Truck Driving Man" were Richard Festinger and Jeffrey Shurtleff, who were members of David Harris' draft resistance organisation. The song was dedicated to the then governor of California, Ronald Reagan, and the lyrics were aimed at the Ku Klux Klan. The penultimate of Baez' numbers was "Swing Low Sweet Chariot", which she performed a capella.

Full Name	Joan Chandos Baez
Known As	Joan Baez
Instruments	Vox, Guitar, Ukulele, Piano
Born	January 9, 1941 Staten Island, New York, USA
Current Age (2019)	78
Genre/Style	Folk, Americana, Folk Rock, Gospel, Country Folk, Latin

THE LINEUP

Saturday Afternoon to Sunday Morning

Quill
Country Joe McDonald
John B. Sebastian
Santana
Keef Hartley Band
The Incredible String Band
Canned Heat
Mountain
Grateful Dead
Creedance Clearwater Revival
Janis Joplin
Sly & the Family Stone
The Who
Jefferson Airplane

QUILL

On Stage
12:15pm - 12:45pm

Playlist
They Live the Life
That's How I Eat
Driftin'
Waitin' for You

When Quill heralded the beginning of the second day at Woodstock, they did so as a hugely popular drawcard. The Boston based band was already famous for an impromptu Manhattan nightclub jam session that featured Jimi Hendrix and Stephen Stills, and the promoters were eager to cash in on their popularity. The torrential rain of the previous night had abated when the group arrived by helicopter, fresh from having played a number of free goodwill gigs on behalf of Woodstock Ventures as a means of satisfying the local authorities. The experimental rock band was led by Dan Cole, who was fighting an infection that required an antibiotic injection from a local doctor, and their four-song set was not without its technical problems. The previous night's rain had affected the synchronisation between the audio track and the filming, making it impossible for them to appear in the film and effectively robbing them of a chance for worldwide promotion and success.

Band Members	Jon Cole - Vox, Bass Dan Cole - Vox, Percussion, Trombone Roger North - Drums, Percussion Norm Rogers - Guitar, Vox, Percussion Phil Thayer - Keyboard, Flute, Saxophone, Percussion
Formed	1967
Genre/Style	Psychedelic Rock, Prog Rock, Art Rock

COUNTRY JOE McDONALD

On Stage
1:00m - 1:30pm

Playlist
Janis
Donovan's Reef
Heartaches by the Number
Ring of Fire
Tennessee Stud
Rockin' Round the World
Flyin' High
I Seen a Rocket
The Fish Cheer/I-Feel-Like-I'm-Fixin'-to-Die Rag

Country Joe McDonald performed both as a solo artist and as part of his own band at Woodstock on separate occasions. His first appearance was on Saturday afternoon as a solo artist, and his appearance had been much anticipated. A prolific songwriter, it was McDonald who captured anti-war sentiment in his famous "I-Feel-Like-I'm-Fixin'-to-Die-Rag" with the catchcry, "And it's one-two-three. What are we fightin' for? Don't ask me, I don't give a damn. Next stop is Vietnam". Country Joe's solo set was generally laid back, with his opening number, "Janis" (he and Janis Joplin had previously dated). Amid the pro-drugs environment at Woodstock, Country Joe was one of a number of artists who publically commented on the inferior quality of the brown acid (LSD). He finished his set with his famous "Fish Cheer", replacing the letters F-I-S-H with F-U-C-K and subsequently launching into the "I-Feel-Like-I'm-Fixin'-to-Die-Rag" after encouraging the crowd with the following words:

"Listen, people; I don't know how you expect to ever stop the war if you can't sing any better than that. There's about three-hundred-thousand of you fuckers out there - I want you to start singing!"

Full Name	Joseph Allen McDonald
Known As	Country Joe McDonald Country Joe
Instruments	Vox, Guitar
Born	January 1, 1942
Current Age (2019)	77
Genre/Style	Country, Country Rock, Alternative Country, Bluegrass, Folk, Psychedelic Rock, Acid Rock

JOHN B. SEBASTIAN

On Stage
3:30pm – 3:55pm

Playlist
How Have You Been
Rainbows All Over Your Blues
I Had a Dream
Darlin' Be Home Soon
Younger Generation

John B. Sebastian was not scheduled to appear at Woodstock, and he had arrived as a spectator only. The ex-Lovin' Spoonful founder was asked to perform an acoustic set as a means of filling in while the sound crew swept water off the stage in preparation for Santana's PA gear. Sebastian agreed, and as he was already high before being asked, his five-song set was filled with laid-back humour as he played. At one point, he also joined in the brown acid commentary, gently suggesting that those concerned about the quality of the LSD take only half a hit. Casual yet talented, Sebastian's impromptu set included three songs from an as-yet unreleased album and two Lovin' Spoonful songs. When asked later about how high he had been during his performance, Sebastian remarked that the atmosphere itself at Woodstock was already naturally high.

Full Name	John Benson Sebastian
Known As	John B. Sebastian G. Pugliese
Instruments	Vox, Guitar, Harmonica, Piano, Autoharp
Born	March 17, 1944 Greenwich Village, New York, USA
Current Age (2019)	75
Genre/Style	Rock, Pop, Blues, Folk

On Stage
2:00pm – 2:45pm

Playlist

Waiting	Jingo
Evil Ways	Persuasion
You Just Don't Care	Soul Sacrifice
Savor	Fried Neckbones and Some Home Fries

Latin rock band Santana was relatively unknown when they performed at Woodstock, with the gig having been secured by Bill Graham (who would become their manager for a time). Graham was asked to assist Woodstock Ventures with planning and logistics, and he did so on the proviso that the new band was added to list of performers. At the time, Santana had been moving away from playing purely Latin music and had been developing their own sound through Carlos Santana's involvement with Sri Chimnoy, a guru. The esoteric Latin rock fusion that resulted formed the nucleus of the band's debut album, and they were already in the studio in May, 1969. Santana's large percussion section was the key to the magical sound that greeted the Woodstock crowd, and the crowd were hugely receptive. When drummer Michael Shrieve launched into a legendary drum solo during their penultimate number, "Soul Sacrifice", the atmosphere was electric. Following their successful Woodstock performance, Santana released their new album. The filming problems encountered during Quill's set had been fixed by that time, so Santana benefitted hugely from the release of the documentary during the following year.

Known As	Santana Santana Blues Band
Band Members	Carlos Santana - Vox, Guitar, Maracas, Cowbell Gregg Rolie - Vox, Keyboards, Tambourine, Maracas, Jingle Bells Jose "Chepito" Areas - Trumpet, Percussion Mike Carabello - Congas Michael Shrieve - Drums David Brown - Bass (Died 2000)
Formed	1956
Genre/Style	Latin Rock, Psychedelic Rock, Blues Rock, Acid Rock, Chicano Rock

Keef Hartley Band

On Stage
4:45pm – 5:30pm

Playlist
Spanish Fly
She's Gone
Too Much Thinkin'
Believe in You
Rock Me Baby
Sinnin' for You / Leaving Trunk / Just to Cry / Sinnin' for You

Rumour has it that the Keef Hartley Band played using Santana's equipment. Headed by drummer Keith Hartley, the band was one of the few British bands to play at Woodstock, and many critics compared them favourably with Blood Sweat and Tears following their performance. The band had completed their album "Halfbreed" and were keen to promote it during the festival, which was an excellent platform for showcasing their blend of jazz, blues and rock & roll. Sadly, the band were not filmed, and no official footage of their performance is available.

Band Members	Keith "Keef" Hartley - Drums (Died 2011)
	Miller Anderson - Guitar, Vox
	Jimmy Jewell - Saxophone
	Henry Lowther - Violin, Trumpet
	Gary Thain - Bass (Died 1975)
Formed	1967
Genre/Style	Jazz/Blues/Rock and Roll Fusion

THE INCREDIBLE STRING BAND

On Stage
6:00pm – 6:30pm

Playlist
Invocation
The Letter
Gather 'Round
This Moment
Come with Me
When You Find Out Who You Are

Part of the progressive, psychedelic British music scene, the Incredible String Band were scheduled to play on the Friday, but they refused due to the torrential rain. As a result, they were very much the psychedelic fish-out-of-water among heavy rock artists, and the crowd had been warming up to the heavier music after Santana and Keef Hartley's band. Creative, artistic and musically innovative, the band struggled to adequately showcase its enormous talent in the new time slot, and their reception was far more lukewarm than it might have been had they played on the Friday as originally scheduled. Additionally, all members of the band were multi-instrumentalists who had been forced to reduce instrument numbers for the gig, so the crowd were not aware of the band's true potential. Due to its unfortunate re-scheduling, the Incredible String Band was not featured in the 1970 film release, but Melanie Safka (who stepped into their Friday spot) was.

Band Members	Mike Heron - Guitar, Piano, Percussion, Vox Robin Williamson - Guitar, Piano, Violin, Vox Christina "Licorice" McKechnie - Percussion, Vox Rose Simpson - Bass, Recorder, Percussion, Vox
Formed	1966
Genre/Style	Psychedelic Folk, Prog Folk, British Folk Rock

On Stage
7:30pm – 8:30pm

Playlist
I'm Her Man
Going Up the Country
A Change Is Gonna Come / Leaving This Town
Too Many Drivers at the Wheel

I Know My Baby

Woodstock Boogie

On the Road Again

Los Angeles group Canned Heat was flown in by helicopter to play their set as the sun was setting. At the time, the band was one of the most popular of their generation, and they had appeared at virtually every major music event in the USA. Known for blues classics as well as their own "psychedelic solos", Canned Heat's two most successful songs (Goin' up the Country and On the Road Again) were modern versions of old blues standards from the first half of the century. With their large following and a crowd who knew they were in for a lengthy set, it was surprising that their performance wasn't included in the 1970 documentary, although the title track of the film was an audio version of "Goin' up the Country. The song was also included in the triple Woodstock album, while "Woodstock Boogie" was included in the Woodstock 2 album.

Band Members	Alan "Blind Owl" Wilson - Vox, Guitar, Harmonica (Died 1970)
	Bob "The Bear" Hite - Vox, Harmonica (Died 1981)
	Larry "The Mole" Taylor - Bass
	Harvey "The Snake" Mandel - Guitar
	Adolfo "Fito" de la Parra - Drums
Formed	1965
Genre/Style	Blues Rock, Boogie Rock

MOUNTAIN

On Stage
9:00pm – 10:00pm

Playlist
Blood of the Sun
Stormy Monday
Theme for an Imaginary Western
Long Red
For Yasgur's Farm (untitled at the time)
Beside the Sea
Waiting to Take You Away
Dreams of Milk and Honey / Guitar Solo
Blind Man
Dirty Shoes Blues
Southbound Train

Hard rock and blues rock band Mountain brought with them a Cream-inspired sound and was enthusiastically received at Woodstock. It was only their fourth gig as a band, and they took their name from lead singer Leslie West's recently released solo album. Their set opener was "Blood of the Sun", followed by the popular "Stormy Monday". The fifth song, now known as "For Yasgur's Farm" is sometimes known as "Who Am I But You and the Sun", but it was Leslie West's guitar solo after "Dreams of Milk and Honey" that totally captured the crowd below the stage. While Mountain were not part of the original Woodstock movie or album, "Blood of the Sun" and "Theme for an Imaginary Western" were included in the second volume, and "Beside the Sea" and "Southbound Train" were included on the 40th Anniversary DVD.

Band Members	Leslie West - Vox, Guitar Steve Knight -Keyboards (Died 2013) Felix Pappalardi - Bass, Vox (Died 1983) Norman D. Smart II - Drums
Formed	1969
Genre/Style	Hard Rock, Blues Rock, Heavy Metal

GRATEFUL DEAD

On Stage

10:30pm – 12:05am

Playlist

St. Stephen

Mama Tried

Dark Star

High Time

Turn on Your Love Light

For The Grateful Dead, Woodstock was not the straightforward gig they might have expected. Instead, their set was plagued with rain-related problems. The band itself was its own unique phenomenon, blending aspects of rock and roll, folk, country, jazz and blues to create what often amounted to a musical party atmosphere. Most of their material was lengthy and included improvised solos and improvised lyrics - in short, a Grateful Dead concert was always a surprise package. Woodstock was not the anticipated party however, and they were delayed as their heavy equipment was too much for the turntable stage and the electrical system needed repairing. When the band finally began, they began receiving electric shocks through the PA system on account of the recent heavy rains. Compounding the electric shocks was the "chilled out" state of the band members themselves, who had trouble comprehending what was happening to them. The result was periods of them not at their best, interspersed with long silences, stoned confusion and a lot of indecipherable banter. They finished at midnight after an epic version of "Turn on Your Lovelight".

Band Members	Jerry Garcia - Guitar, Pedal Steel, Banjo, Vox (Died 1995)
	Bob Weir - Guitar, Vox
	Phil Lesh - Bass Guitar, Trumpet, Vox
	Bill Kreutzman - Drums, Percussion
	Mickey Hart - Drums, Percussion
	Ron "Pigpen" McKernan - Vox, Harmonica, Organ (Died 1973)
	Tom Constanten - Organ, Piano
Formed	1965
Genre/Style	Rock

CREEDENCE CLEARWATER REVIVAL

On Stage
12:30am – 1:20am

Playlist

Born on the Bayou
Green River
Ninety-Nine and a Half (Won't Do)
Commotion
Bootleg
Bad Moon Rising

Proud Mary
I Put a Spell on You
Night Time Is the Right Time
Keep on Chooglin'
Susie Q

The problems encountered by The Grateful Dead resulted in Creedence Clearwater Revival facing a wet, muddy and sleeping audience when they began their Woodstock set. According to front man John Fogerty, the scene below him was, "... *just bodies from hell; all intertwined and asleep; all covered in mud .....*" The first band booked for Woodstock began its set upbeat, watching as the sleeping audience came back to life and others re-emerged from cars, vans, bedrolls, tents and makeshift shelters. Playing material from the first of their three hugely popular albums (Willy and the Poor Boys was not released until November, 1969), they re-animated the festival at a faster than usual tempo. Once "I put a Spell on You" began, the tempo slowed, and "Keep on Choogin'" lasted for a sensational nine minutes. Creedence finished their Woodstock set with "Suzi Q" as an encore and had a ten minute jam session before retiring. Although John Fogerty did not allow the footage to be used for the 1970 film release on the basis that it was not their finest gig, most of those who were there believed it to be the highlight of the festival.

Band Members	John Fogerty - Vox, Guitar, Harmonica
	Tom Fogerty - Vox, Rhythm Guitar (Died 1990)
	Doug "Cosmo" Clifford - Drums
	Stu Cook - Bass, Keyboard
Formed	1967
Genre/Style	Roots Rock, Country Rock, Swamp Rock

JANIS JOPLIN

On Stage

2:00am – 3:00am

Playlist

Raise Your Hand

As Good As You've Been to This World

To Love Somebody

Summertime

Try (Just a Little Bit Harder)

Kozmic Blues

Can't Turn You Loose

Work Me, Lord

Piece of My Heart

Ball an' Chain

When Janis Joplin and her band were flown in by helicopter on Saturday afternoon, Joplin was blown away by the size of the Woodstock - so much so that she was unable to answer any questions fielded by the Press. Her nervousness increased as the band awaited their turn (which took ten hours), and Joplin drank and shot heroin to cope. Not at her best, Joplin was nevertheless mesmerising as she and the band performed numbers from her "I Got Dem Ol' Kozmic Blues Again Mama!" album. The numbers considered to be the highlight of her performance were "Summertime" and "Work Me, Lord". Joplin responded to two calls for an encore - the first being "Piece of My Heart" and the last "Ball an' Chain". Her performance over, Joplin remained at Woodstock for the duration and can be seen standing in a circle behind Crosby, Stills & Nash as they performed on the Sunday night/Monday morning. According to Joan Baez, she and Joplin sat together in Joe Cocker's van to watch Hendrix close the festival. A little over 12 months later, both Joplin and Hendrix would be dead.

Full Name	Janis Lyn Joplin
Known As	Janis Joplin Pearl
Instruments	Vox
Born	January 19, 1943 Port Arthur, Texas, USA
Died	October 4, 1970 Los Angeles, California, USA
Age at Death	27
Genre/Style	Psychedelic Rock, Soul Blues

SLY & THE FAMILY STONE

On Stage
3:30am – 4:20am
Playlist

M'Lady

Sing a Simple Song

You Can Make It If You Try

Everyday People

Dance To The Music

Music Lover

I Want to Take You Higher

Love City

Stand!

San Francisco based Sly and the Family Stone had a No. 1 hit in 1968 with their single, "Everyday People", and they were the first US rock band to include racially integrated members. Their hit single was an anti-prejudice song and popularised the phrase, "Different strokes for different folks". When the band stepped on stage for their Woodstock set, they did so looking and sounding fresh and alive, and their set was one of the festival's most popular. They had previously played at the Harlem Cultural Festival three weeks prior, using what became known as the "Black Woodstock" as a dress rehearsal for the latter event. The set list was comprised mainly of songs from their album, "Stand!", which had been released in May, 1969, and two of the numbers (Music Lover and I Want to Take You Higher) each lasted for over ten minutes.

Band Members	Sly Stone - Vox, Keyboard, Harmonica
	Rose Stone - Vox, Keyboards
	Freddie Stone - Vox, Guitar
	Cynthia Robinson - Trumpet (Died 2015)
	Greg Errico - Drums
	Larry Graham - Bass
	Jerry Martini - Saxophone
Formed	1966
Genre/Style	Psychedelic Soul, Rock, Funk

The WHO

On Stage

5:00am – 6:05am

Playlist

Heaven and Hell	Pinball Wizard	See Me, Feel Me
I Can't Explain	Do You Think It's Alright?	Summertime Blues
It's a Boy	Fiddle About	Shakin' All Over
1921	There's a Doctor	My Generation
Amazing Journey	Go to the Mirror	Naked Eye (instrumental)
Sparks"	Smash the Mirror	
Eyesight to the Blind	I'm Free	
Christmas	Tommy's Holiday Camp	
Acid Queen	We're Not Gonna Take It	

The Who had been scheduled to play on the Saturday, but rain and technical delays meant that they didn't step on stage until five o'clock on Sunday morning. Their set was comprised of most of their rock opera album, "Tommy". Initially reluctant to appear at Woodstock, the British band demanded their $13,000 payment in advance and later declared their gig one of the worst they'd played. One of the major problems encountered by the band was the interruption of their set following "Pinball Wizard". At that point, activist Abbie Hoffman rushed on stage, grabbed the microphone and began a political tirade against the jailing of a member of the White Panther Party. He yelled at the audience, "...*this is a pile of shit while John Sinclair rots in prison!*", incensing Pete Townshend, who was adjusting his amp. Townshend (who agreed with Hoffman about the wrongful imprisonment of Sinclair) was nevertheless furious at having had the sanctity of the stage violated and voiced his anger at Hoffman. "*Fuck off! Fuck off my fucking stage!*" he yelled. Some sources state that Townshend then ran at Hoffman and hit him in the back, but there was no film taken to support or refute the incident.

Band Members	Roger Daltrey - Vox
	Pete Townsend - Vox, Guitar
	John Entwhistle - Vox, Bass (Died 2002)
	Keith Moon - Drums (Died 1978)
Formed	1964
Genre/Style	Rock, Hard Rock, Power Pop

JEFFERSON AIRPLANE

On Stage
8:00am – 9:40am

Playlist

The Other Side of This Life

Somebody to Love

3/5 of a Mile in 10 Seconds

Won't You Try/Saturday Afternoon

Eskimo Blue Day

Plastic Fantastic Lover

Wooden Ships

Uncle Sam's Blues

Volunteers

The Ballad of You and Me and Pooneil

Come Back Baby

White Rabbit

The House at Pooneil Corners

Jefferson Airplane were already widely popular when they appeared at Woodstock, having headlined at Monterey in 1967 and been part of the "Summer of Love". The psychedelic rock band were the epitome of the young, groovy, free-loving hippie set, and their music spoke for an entire generation. Grace Slick began the set by announcing, "*Alright, friends; you have seen the heavy groups, now you will see morning maniac music, believe me. Yeah! It's the new dawn!*" The band launched into what was considered a standard set for them for the first six songs, but included a surprising rendition of "Wooden Ships" that lasted for well over 20 minutes. The anti-war song, "Uncle Sam's Blues" followed with only Jorma Kaukonen singing, and "Volunteers" was next (and would become an unofficial Woodstock anthem). The band, who had recruited British session muso Nicky Hopkins to play keyboards at Woodstock, then performed the 15-minute long "The Ballad of You and Me and Pooneil", which featured a huge bass solo by Jack Casady. Three songs later, Woodstock's Saturday program finally came to an end at 9:40am on Sunday.

Band Members	Marty Balin - Vox, Maracas, Tambourine Grace Slick - Vox, Maracas, Tambourine Paul Kantner - Guitar, Vox (Died 2016) Jorma Kaukonen - Guitar, Vox Jack Casady - Bass Spencer Dryden - Drums (Died 2005) Nicky Hopkins - Piano (Died 1994)
Formed	1965
Genre/Style	Psychedelic Rock, Folk Rock, Acid Rock

THE LINEUP

Sunday Afternoon to Monday Morning

Joe Cocker & the Grease Band
Country Joe and the Fish
Ten Years After
The Band
Johnny Winter
Blood, Sweat & Tears
Crosby, Stills, Nash & Young
Paul Butterfield Blues Band
Sha Na Na
Jimi Hendrix - Jimi Hendrix / Gypsy Sun & Rainbows

JOE COCKER

On Stage
2:00 pm – 3:25 pm

Playlist

Instrumental Jam	Do I Still Figure in Your Life	I Shall Be Released
Who Knows What Tomorrow May Bring	Feelin' Alright	Hitchcock Railway
	Just Like a Woman	Something to Say
Dear Landlord	Let's Go Get Stoned	With a Little Help from My Friends
Something Comin' On	I Don't Need a Doctor	

For those who were there, Joe Cocker's rendition of "With a Little Help From My Friends" was one of the highlights of the Woodstock festival. For many music lovers in the USA, the name of Joe Cocker was unknown before August, 1969, but he already had a No. 1 hit on the British charts with his soulful version of The Beatles' song and was a must-have as far as the organisers were concerned. The set began with two instrumental numbers without Joe Cocker as a warm up for the band (and the audience), and Cocker began his set with "Dear Landlord". Throughout the set, the weather threatened ominously, but it held off long enough for Cocker to showcase his somewhat strange trademark movements and his exceptional talent at totally owning a cover (regardless of the original artist). The gravelly vocals and fat band sound captured the hearts and minds of hundreds of thousands of music lovers at Woodstock, and as though on cue, a massive thunderstorm broke out after Joe Cocker and the Grease Band had finished.

Full Name	John Robert Cocker
Known As	Joe Cocker
	The Sheffield Soul Shouter
	Vance Arnold
Instruments	Vox, Piano, Harmonica
Born	20 May, 1944
	Sheffield, Yorkshire, England
Died	22 December, 2014
	Crawford, Colorado, USA
Age at Death	70
Genre/Style	Blues, Rock, Pop, Soul

COUNTRY JOE AND THE FISH

On Stage
6:30 pm – 8:00 pm

Playlist

Rock & Soul Music

(Thing Called) Love

Not So Sweet Martha Lorraine

Sing, Sing, Sing

Summer Dresses

Friend, Lover, Woman, Wife

Silver and Gold

Maria

Love Machine

Ever Since You Told Me That You Love Me

Short Jam (instrumental)

Crystal Blues

Rock & Soul Music

The "Fish"

Three hours after Joe Cocker and the Grease Band completed their set, the weather cleared and allowed a return to the Woodstock stage on the festival's final day. Country Joe McDonald, who had performed as a solo act the previous day, returned with his band, Country Joe and the Fish. The band had been recruited as a replacement to British band Jethro Tull, who had turned down their invitation to perform. By that stage in their careers, McDonald and his band were beginning to embrace a more Pop sound, and the organ featured strongly in their set. The performance itself was considered a little flat by critics of the time, but it might well have been thought of even flatter had they performed immediately following Joe Cocker's set. As it had been with McDonald on the previous day, the set finished with the "F-I-S-H Cheer", which naturally became the "F-U-C-K Cheer" and enlivened an outdoor audience still recovering from an earlier thunderstorm..

Band Members	Country Joe McDonald - Vox, Guitar, Harmonica, Kazoo
	Barry "The Fish" Melton - Lead Guitar, Vox
	Gregory Leroy Dewey - Drums
	Mark Kapner - Keyboards, Organ
	Doug Metzner - Bass
Formed	1965
Genre/Style	Psychedelic Rock, Folk Rock, Acid Rock

Ten Years After

On Stage
8:15 pm – 9:15 pm

Playlist
Spoonful
Good Morning Little Schoolgirl
Hobbit
I Can't Keep from Crying Sometimes
Help Me
I'm Going Home

Ten Years After was a British heavy blues/rock band renowned for its lengthy guitar and drum solos. They had already performed at the Newport Jazz Festival and the Seattle Pop Festival in July of 1969, and their on-stage intensity had resulted in a huge following in the USA. As a result, their appearance at Woodstock was a much anticipated one. While technical problems resulted in a less than world-changing performance, Ten Years After nevertheless produced a memorable set. The earlier thunderstorm had produced high humidity, which affected the band's instruments and caused them to constantly go out of tune. The set was interspersed with musicians constantly re-tuning, but it did not rob them of the chance to capture the Woodstock crowd with their final 12-minute number, "I'm Going Home". Captured on film, the performance catapulted the group to stardom long after their technically frustrating gig was over.

Band Members	Alvin Lee (Died 2013) - Vox, Guitar
	Leo Lyons - Bass
	Chick Churchill - Organ
	Ric Lee - Drums
Formed	1966
Genre/Style	Hard Rock, Blues Rock

The Band

On Stage
10:00 pm – 10:50 pm

Playlist
Chest Fever
Don't Do It
Tears of Rage
We Can Talk
Long Black Veil
Don't You Tell Henry
Ain't No More Cane
This Wheel's on Fire
I Shall Be Released
The Weight
Loving You Is Sweeter Than Ever

The Canadian-American group "The Band" had formed in the early 1960s as a backing band for Rockabilly singer Ronnie Hawkins. Known at one time as "The Hawks", they rose to prominence in 1965 when Bob Dylan hired them for his 1965 USA Tour and his 1966 World Tour. Dylan and The Band made informal recordings in New York in 1967, and the work eventually became "The Basement Tapes". In 1968, the group began performing as "The Band" in their own right and released the first of what would culminate in ten studio albums. With a single album behind them, they played seven of the album's 11 songs at Woodstock. The last song performed before the encore was "The Weight", which had become famous as part of the "Easy Rider" soundtrack and was a huge hit with the Woodstock crowd.

Band Members	Robbie Robertson - Vox, Guitar
	Rick Danko (Died 1999) - Bass, Vox
	Levon Helm (Died 2012) - Drums, Mandolin, Vox
	Garth Hudson - Piano, Organ, Synthesiser, Sax, Clavinet
	Richard Manuel (Died 1986) - Piano, Organ, Drums, Vox
Formed	1968
Genre/Style	Folk Rock, Roots Rock, Americana, Country Rock

JOHNNY WINTER

On Stage

12:00 am – 1:05 am

Playlist

Mama, Talk to Your Daughter

Leland Mississippi Blues

Mean Town Blues

You Done Lost Your Good Thing Now / Mean Mistreater

I Can't Stand It (with Edgar Winter)

Tobacco Road (with Edgar Winter)

Tell the Truth (with Edgar Winter)

Johnny B. Goode

Johnny Winter was the consummate blues guitarist who worked with Muddy Waters and would eventually become a multi-Grammy winner. For a little over an hour, Winter electrified the Woodstock audience with his mind-blowing solos, slide guitar and signature blues riffs that came together to showcase his amazing talent. Three of the songs were performed with Edgar Winter (Johnny's brother) on sax and keyboard mixing things up with a jazz flavour, and Edgar provided vocals for "Tobacco Road". Cover versions of Bo Diddley and B. B. King numbers were lengthy but exciting, and Winter's encore was his own version of Chuck Berry's "Johnny B. Goode". Fans of Winter prior to Woodstock were wowed by live versions of "Leland Mississippi Blues", "Mean Town Blues" and "Mean Mistreater" from his first two albums.

Full Name	John Dawson Winter III
Known As	Johnny Winter
Instruments	Guitar, Vox
Born	February 23, 1944 Beaumont, Texas, USA
Died	July 16, 2014 Zurich, Switzerland
Age at Death	70
Genre/Style	Blues, Blues Rock, Rock and Roll, Texas Blues
Backed by	Edgar Winter - Vox, Keyboards, Alto Sax Tommy Shannon - Bass "Uncle" John Turner (Died 2007) - Drums

BLOOD, SWEAT & TEARS

On Stage
1:30 am – 2:30 am

Playlist

More and More

Just One Smile

Something's Coming On

More Than You'll Ever Know

Spinning Wheel

Sometimes in Winter

Smiling Phases

God Bless the Child

I Stand Accused

And When I Die

You've Made Me So Very Happy

Originally from New York City, Blood, Sweat and Tears was already hugely popular when they appeared at Woodstock. Renowned for their huge on-stage presence, the band added yet another facet to the already diverse music at Woodstock. The band's founder, Al Kooper, had already moved on from the band, and vocalist David Clayton-Thomas was at the helm. Their self titled 1968 album would ultimately surpass The Beatles' "Abbey Road" to win Album of the Year at the 1970 Grammy Awards. Unlike a number of earlier performers, Blood, Sweat and Tears were not plagued by technical problems, and their set was beautifully delivered. The list included numbers from two previous albums and were virtually flawless in their delivery. Sadly for those fans who were not at Woodstock, the film crew were only able to record the band's opening number before their manager ordered the filming to stop as they had not been paid to have their performance filmed.

Band Members	David Clayton-Thomas - Vox Bobby Colomby - Drums Jim Fielder - Bass Dick Halligan - Keyboards, Flute, Trombone Jerry Hyman - Trombone, Recorder Steve Katz - Vox, Guitar, Harmonica Lew Soloff (Died 2015) - Trumpet - Flugelhorn Fred Lipsius - Piano, Alto Sax Chuck Winfield - Trumpet, Flugelhorn
Formed	1967
Genre/Style	Psychedelic Rock, Jazz Rock, R&B, Pop Rock

CROSBY, STILLS, NASH (& YOUNG)

On Stage
3:00 am – 4:00 am

Playlist

Judy Blue Eyes	Wonderin'	Wooden Ships
Blackbird	You Don't Have to Cry	**Acoustic Encores**
Helplessly Hoping	**Electric Set**	Find the Cost of Freedom
Guinnevere	Pre-Road Downs	49 Bye-Byes
Marrakesh Express	Long Time Gone	
4 + 20	Bluebird	
Mr. Soul	Sea of Madness	

In 1968, David Crosby (the Byrds), Stephen Stills (Buffalo Springfield) and Graham Nash (the Hollies) formed themselves into a group, and by July, 1969, had produced an album simply entitled, "Crosby, Stills & Nash". Stills had played with Neil Young in Buffalo Springfield, and he introduced him to the others as a fourth artist to join them for their Woodstock gig. The quartet played together once before the festival and according to Stephen Stills, they were "scared shitless" about playing in front of an audience. Their set was split into electric and acoustic sections, and the Crosby, Stills & Nash trio played the first six songs. Neil Young then arrived and joined Stephen Stills to perform "Mr. Soul" and "Wonderin'" as a duo from their Buffalo Springfield days. For the electric set, Young joined the others but refused to be filmed as he found it distracting. As a result, many fans watching the 1970 movie release were not aware that Neil Young was even at Woodstock.

Band Members	David Crosby - Guitar, Vox
	Stephen Stills - Guitar, Vox, Piano, Organ, Percussion
	Graham Nash - Guitar, Vox, Organ, Percussion
	Neil Young - Guitar, Vox, Piano, Organ
	Greg Reeves - Bass
	Dallas Taylor (Died 2015) - Drums
Formed	1968
Genre/Style	Folk Rock, Soft Rock, Country Rock

PAUL BUTTERFIELD BLUES BAND

On Stage
6:00 am – 6:45 am

Playlist
Born Under a Bad Sign
No Amount of Loving
Driftin'
Morning Sunrise
All in a Day
Love March
Everything's Gonna Be Alright

The Paul Butterfield Blues Band was a Chicago blues band in the process of embracing a more soul-influenced feel when they performed at Woodstock in 1969. With horns and sax dominating, they had been invited to perform at the festival on the strength of albums released in 1965 and 1966, an appearance at the 1967 Monterey Pop Festival and recording work they had undertaken with Muddy Waters at Chicago's Auditorium Theater in April, 1969. None of their seven songs appeared in the 1970 film, but their sixth number, "Love March", featured on the 1970 album. Although the performance was a good one, the band that performed at Woodstock was markedly different from the one seen at Monterey two years previously. As it turned out, Woodstock was the pinnacle of the band's career, but what a way to peak!

Band Members	Paul Butterfield (Died 1987) - Vox, Harmonica
	Howard "Buzzy" Feiten - Guitar
	Rod Hicks (Died 2013) - Bass
	Ted Harris - Keyboards
	Phillip Wilson (Died 1992) - Drums
	Steve Madaio - Trumpet, Percussion
	Keith Johnson - Trumpet, Percussion
	David Sanborn - Alto Sax, Percussion
	Trevor Lawrence - Baritone Sax, Percussion
	Gene Dinwiddie (Died 2002) - Tenor Sax, Percussion, Vox
Formed	Early 1960s
Genre/Style	Chicago Blues, Blues Rock

Sha Na Na

On Stage
7:30 am – 8:00 am

Playlist

Get a Job	Jailhouse Rock	Little Darlin'
Come Go with Me	Wipe Out	At the Hop
Silhouettes	Blue Moon	Duke of Earl
Teen Angel	(Who Wrote) The Book of Love	Get a Job (Reprise)

It was Jimi Hendrix who suggested Sha-Na-Na as a possible Woodstock act, having seen the group perform at Steve Paul's Scene Club earlier in the year. The group was a fifties Rock and Roll act that featured dancing and Doo-Wop, and it was a generation away from the Summer of Love people at Woodstock. Nevertheless, the group was booked to precede Hendrix and were a hit with the crowd. Colourful costuming, exceptional harmonies and energetic dancing electrified many of those waiting for Hendrix to appear, and when they appeared in the 1970 film, their presence sparked the fifties revival that would dominate much of the decade. That revival would ultimately deliver films such as American Graffiti and Grease to audiences of the late 1970s, as well as the "Happy Days" TV series.

Band Members	Joe Witkin - Vox, Keyboards
	Jocko Marcellino - Drums
	Donald "Donny" York - Vox
	Rob Leonard - Vox
	Alan Cooper - Vox
	Frederick "Dennis" Greene (Died 2015) - Vox
	Dave Garrett - Vox
	Richard "Richie" Joffe - Vox
	Scott Powell - Vox
	Henry Gross - Guitar
	Bruce Clarke III - Bass
	Elliot Cahn - Rhythm Guitar, Vox
Formed	1969
Genre/Style	Doo Wop, Rock and Roll

JIMI HENDRIX

On Stage

9:00 am – 11:10 am

Playlist

Message to Love	Foxy Lady	Stepping Stone
Hear My Train a-Comin'	Jam Back at the House	Star Spangled banner
Spanish Castle Magic	Izabella	Purple Haze
Red House	Gypsy Woman	Woodstock Improvisation
Mastermind	Fire	Villanova junction
Lover Man	Voodoo Child	Hey Joe

By the time Jimi Hendrix' much anticipated set was announced, half of the 400,000 strong crowd had left Woodstock due to the time delay over the three days. Initially introduced by Chip Monck as "The Jimi Hendrix Experience", it was Hendrix who corrected the name by referring to his backing band as "Gypsy Sun and Rainbows". Originally, the headline act was to have performed on the Sunday night, but rain and technical issues had pushed the time into Monday morning and robbed many festival-goers of the opportunity to see their guitar hero. The set began with many of Hendrix' older songs and built up to deliver the incredible "Star Spangled Banner" anthem that electrified fans in person and later on film. Hendrix' guitar work included stunning mimicry of gunfire, rockets and bombs later in the piece, which then burst into "Purple Haze" to the delight and shock of those listening. His "Woodstock Improvisation" remains a favourite of Hendrix purists, and his encore was "Hey Joe". Perhaps one of the most regrettable moments for those who mourned his death a little over 12 months later was when Hendrix announced "Valleys of Neptune" before changing his mind as he "*forgot the words*". The latter was released posthumously as an instrumental work, so the forgotten lyrics remain a mystery to this day.

Full Name	Johnny Allen Hendrix
Known As	Jimi Hendrix
Instruments	Guitar, Vox
Born	November 27, 1942 Seattle, Washington, USA
Died	September 18, 1970 Kensington, London, England
Age at Death	27
Genre/Style	Blues, Rock, Psychedelic Rock, Hard Rock, R&B
Gypsy Sun & Rainbows	Billy Cox - Bass Larry Lee (Died 2007) - Rhythm Guitar, Vox Mitch Mitchell (Died 2008) - Drums Juma Sultan - Congas Gerardo "Jerry" Velez - Congas

Legacy and Aftermath

In the News

In 1969, live television was limited and very few reporters travelled to cover Woodstock. Most of the media reporting focussed on the difficulties experienced by those travelling in the area. Headlines such as, "Hippies Mired in a Sea of Mud" and "Traffic Uptight at Hippiefest" dominated, as did an editorial in the New York times entitled, "Nightmare in the Catskills". The latter publication had earlier reported on the festival's move from Wallkill to Bethel. The area's daily newspaper (Times Herald-Record) published a Saturday version of its paper for festival goers, and used a motorcyclist to get pictures back to the office some 35 miles away. By the time the festival was almost over, the naysayers had been silenced by reports of cooperation, generosity and the generally nice demeanour of those attending. Once the festival had ended, Barnard Collier of the New York Times reported on the exodus of 400,000 people from the Bethel site and stressed the lack of violence that the authorities had been expecting.

On Film

When Artie Kornfield first fielded the idea of a documentary on the Woodstock festival, all but one studio turned him down. However, Fred Weintraub of Warner Bros. ignored his colleagues and paid Kornfield $100,000 to go ahead and make the film. At the time, Warner Bros. was in trouble and on the verge of collapse, so Weintraub put both the future of the studio and his own future on the line. Director Michael Wadleigh headed a crew of 100 New York based workers who agreed to take no money for their work if the film bombed, but double their normal pay if the film was a success. As it turned out, the documentary, "Woodstock" was a hit with audiences around the world and was awarded the Academy Award for Documentary Feature. It also proved to be the saving of Warner Bros. and Woodstock Ventures, the latter having lost money when the festival became a free one.

On Vinyl

The first soundtrack to be released was "Woodstock: Music from the Original Soundtrack and More" as a three-LP set. In the following year, "Woodstock 2" was released. Later releases on CD include:

1994   Woodstock Diary

1994   Jimi Hendrix: Woodstock

1994   Woodstock: Three Days of Peace and Music

1999   Jimi Hendrix: Live at Woodstock

2009   Joe Cocker: Live at Woodstock

2009   The Woodstock Experience

2009   Woodstock: 40 Years on: Back to Yasgur's Farm

Yasgur's Farm and the Bethel Community

Max Yasgur was approached to rent out his farm again the following year for a Woodstock revival, but he refused. He died in 1973.

The residents of Bethel voted out the man who had allowed the festival to be held on their doorsteps, and both the Town of Bethel and New York State passed new mass gathering laws to prevent a repeat of Woodstock. Collectively, local farmers brought 80 lawsuits against the promoters. Those suits and the company's debt were paid for by proceeds from the movie. Over time, the residents of Bethel have come to embrace the legacy of the festival, but their opposition saw the nearby town of Woodstock cash in on the aftermath.

In 1996, Yasgur's Farm and 1,400 acres surrounding it were purchased by Alan Gerry to become the home of the Bethel Woods Center for the Arts. The complex officially opened in July, 2006. During the following month, Crosby, Stills, Nash & Young performed for 16,000 fans 37 years after their Woodstock performance.

Most poignantly, Richie Havens' ashes were scattered at the site on August 18, 2013.

The 40th Anniversary

On August 15, 2009, the Bethel Woods Center for the Arts played host to an eight-hour concert marking the 40th anniversary of the festival. The host for the day was Country Joe McDonald and artists included Big Brother and the Holding Company (playing Janis Joplin's hits), Ten Years After, Canned Heat, Mountain, Jefferson Starship and others.

WOODSTOCK QUOTES

When it comes to quotes about Woodstock, there is not a musician or artist of the era who didn't have something to say about the festival that became one of the most significant cultural events of the 20th century. Here are a few:

Joan Baez
I hope David can hear it (referring to her husband, David Harris, who was in prison for draft resistance at the time).

John Fogerty
We were ready to rock out and we waited and waited and finally it was our turn... ...there were a half million people asleep. These people were out. It was sort of like a painting of a Dante scene, just bodies from hell, all intertwined and asleep, covered with mud ...... And this is the moment I will never forget as long as I live: a quarter mile away in the darkness, on the other edge of this bowl, there was some guy flicking his Bic, and in the night I hear, *'Don't worry about it John. We're with you.'* I played the rest of the show for that guy."

Melanie Safka
[Chip Monck] said that if you lit candles, it would help to keep the rain away. By the time I finished my set, the whole hillside was a mass of little flickering lights. It was an amazing experience to be there, to be in that time and live through that group of people who were acknowledging each other, as if we were all in one family. Woodstock was an affirmation that we were part of each other.

Jimi Hendrix (In a poem he wrote in late 1969)
500,000 halos outshined the mud and history. We washed and drank in God's tears of joy. And for once, and for everyone, the truth was not still a mystery.

John Sebastian
But, what did happen is I went to Woodstock as a member of the audience. I did not show up there with a road manager and a couple of guitars. I showed up with a change of clothes and a toothbrush.

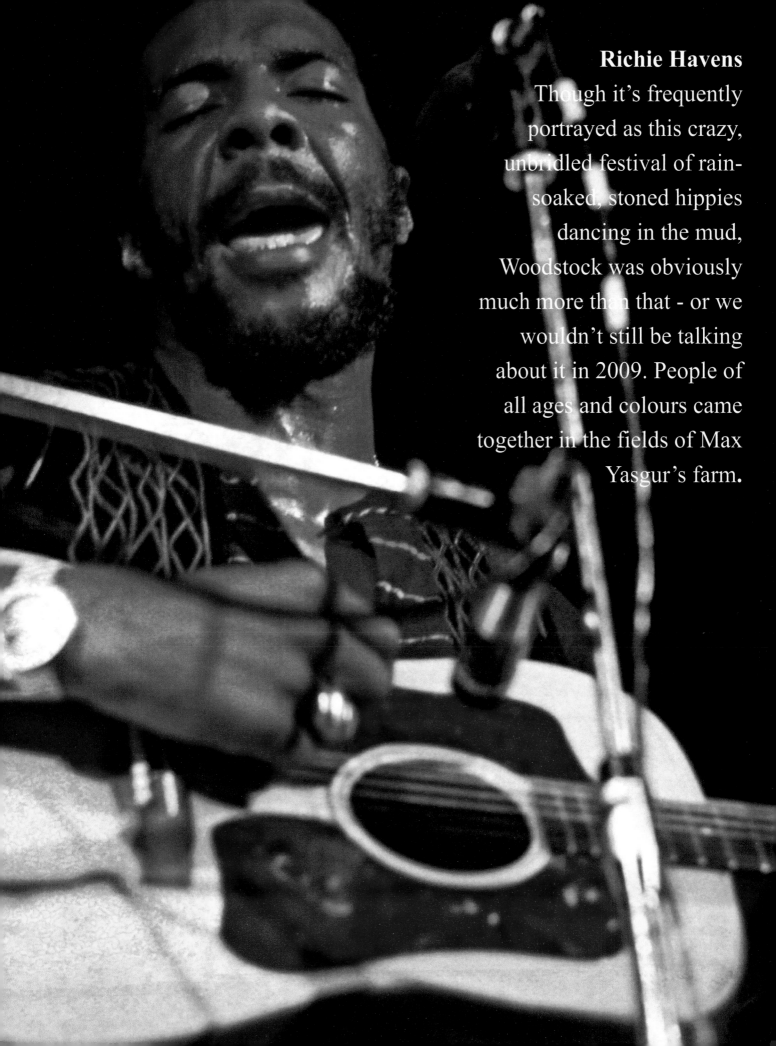

Richie Havens
Though it's frequently portrayed as this crazy, unbridled festival of rain-soaked, stoned hippies dancing in the mud, Woodstock was obviously much more than that - or we wouldn't still be talking about it in 2009. People of all ages and colours came together in the fields of Max Yasgur's farm.

Grace Slick

The fact that nobody got killed at Woodstock is amazing because that was half a million people. We only had 300,000 at Altamont.

Edgar Winter
But when I played Woodstock, I'll never forget that moment looking out over the hundreds of thousands of people, the sea of humanity, seeing all those people united in such a unique way. It just touched me in a way that I'll never forget.

WHO WASN'T THERE

A number of known and unknown names were either overlooked or declined an invitation to perform at Woodstock. Flies on walls aside, we shall never know what went through the minds of those who regretted their omission or declined invitation, but speculation continues today as to what an appearance might have meant to some. The following list covers the majority of those who missed the opportunity or declined the invitation:

Beatles A number of stories exist in relation to The Beatles' absence from Woodstock. One has John Lennon demanding an invitation for Yoko Ono's Plastic Ono Band and being refused, and another has Lennon stuck in Canada an unable to secure a visa to enter the USA.

Bob Dylan A resident of Woodstock, Dylan sailed for England on the first day of the festival, having been booked for the British "Isle of Wight Festival". According to some sources, the singer/songwriter had not welcomed the arrival of thousands of hippies in the area.

Byrds The Byrds declined their invitation to perform at Woodstock as they assumed it would be similar to a number of other American festivals. Additionally, the festival had been presented as a gig in upstate New York with a question mark over payment. The entire band opted for a rest instead.

Chicago Chicago were on the initial list of those who had been signed to play at Woodstock. Bill Graham, a concert promoter, then moved the band's gig dates around so that Santana (who he managed at the time) were able to attend Woodstock instead.

Doors The Doors cancelled their appearance, citing problems encountered at the Monterey Pop Festival as a reason not to attend Woodstock.

Frank Zappa Frank Zappa and his band, Mothers of Invention, turned down their invitation.

Free Free declined their invitation to perform at Woodstock but played at the British Isle of Wight Festival in the following week.

Iron Butterfly Iron Butterfly was to perform at Woodstock, but they were stuck at LaGuardia Airport. They sent an imperious telegram to John Morris (the production coordinator) demanding a helicopter. Morris sent back an acrostic telegram that left the band in no doubt that they were no longer welcome. *For reasons I can't go into / Until you are here / Clarifying your situation / Knowing you are having problems / You will have to find / Other transportation / Unless you plan not to come.*

The Beatles

The Beatles promoters contacted John Lennon to discuss a Beatles performance at Woodstock. Lennon said that the Beatles would not play unless there was also a spot at the festival for Yoko Ono's Plastic Ono Band. He was turned down.

WOODSTOCK PEACE & LOVE MUSIC

Reflection

Reflections

Reflections

WOODSTOCK PEACE & LOVE MUSIC

Reflections

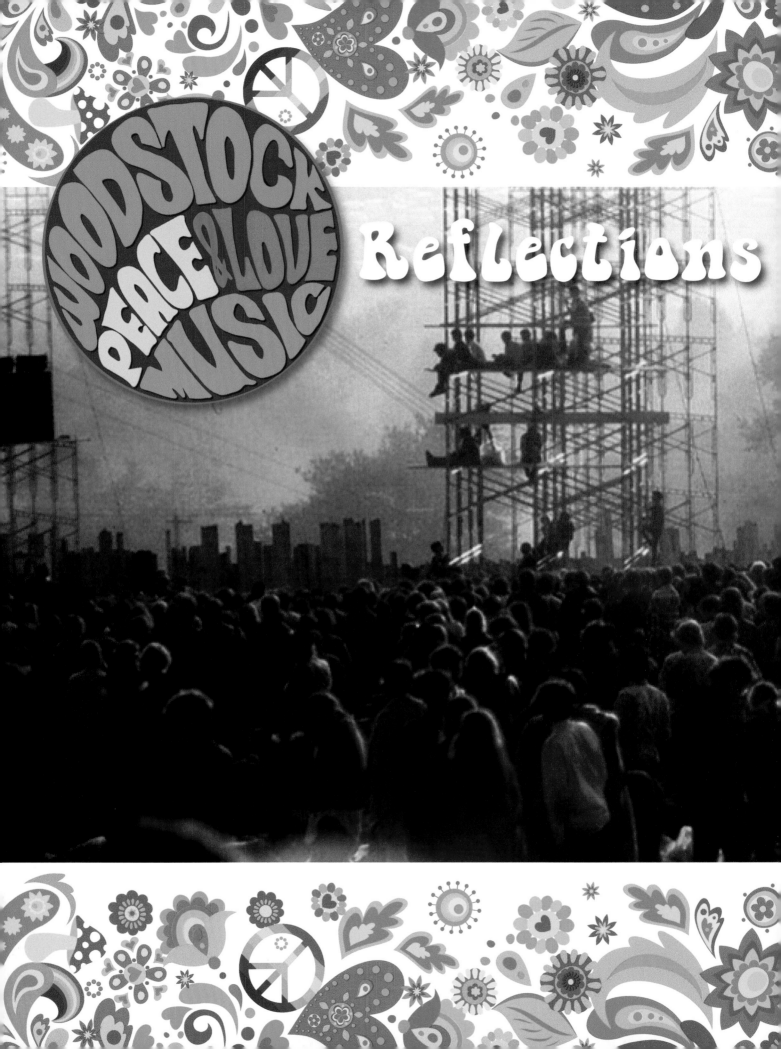

Reflections

Reflections

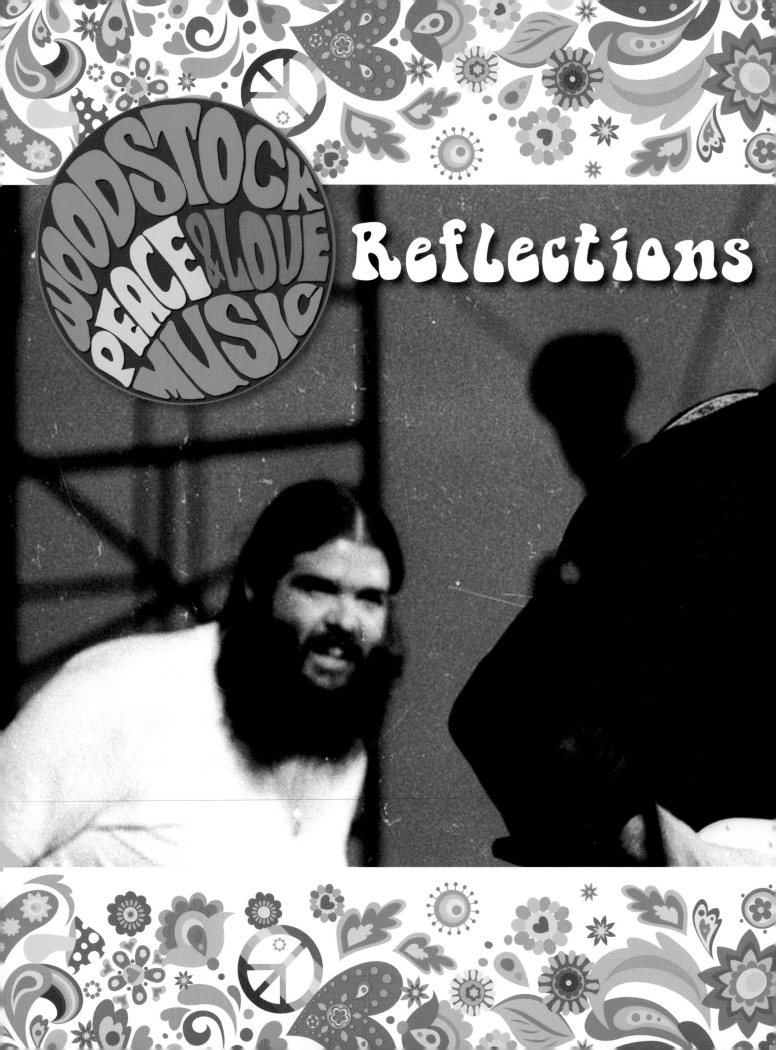

Reflections

Reflections

Reflections

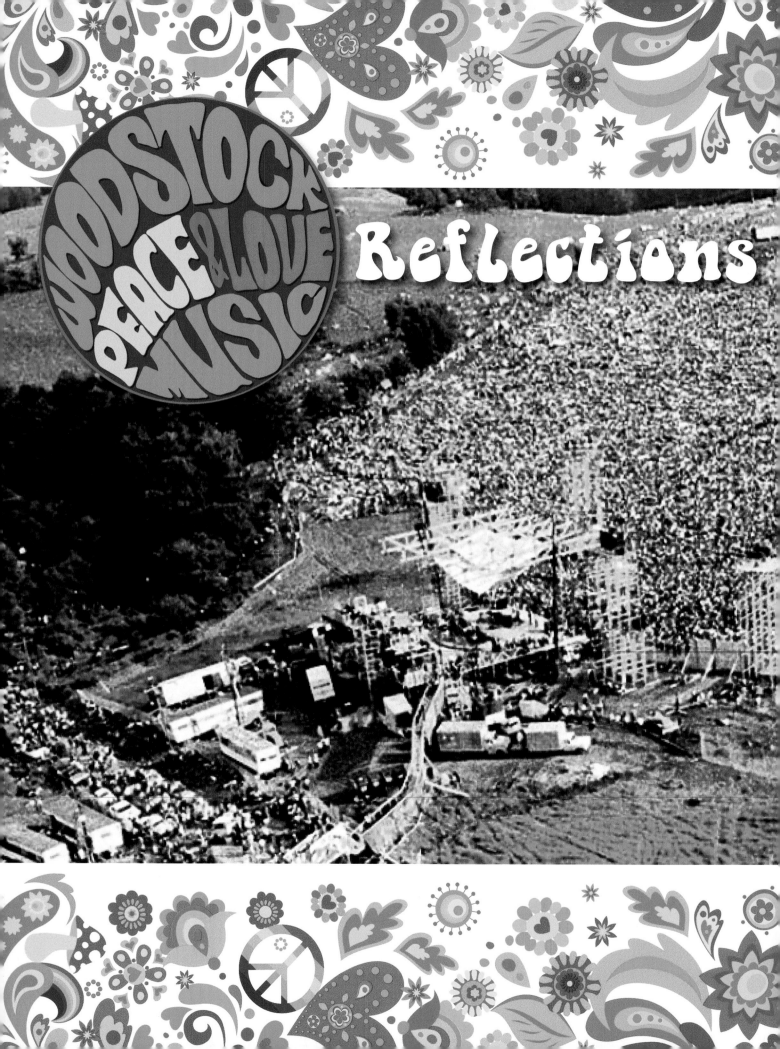

WOODSTOCK PEACE & LOVE MUSIC

Reflections

WOODSTOCK PEACE & LOVE MUSIC

Reflections

WOODSTOCK PEACE & LOVE MUSIC

Reflecti

WOODSTOCK PEACE & LOVE MUSIC

Reflections

WOODSTOCK PEACE & LOVE MUSIC

Reflections

Reflections

WOODSTOCK PEACE & LOVE MUSIC

Reflections

Reflections

WOODSTOCK PEACE & LOVE MUSIC

Reflection

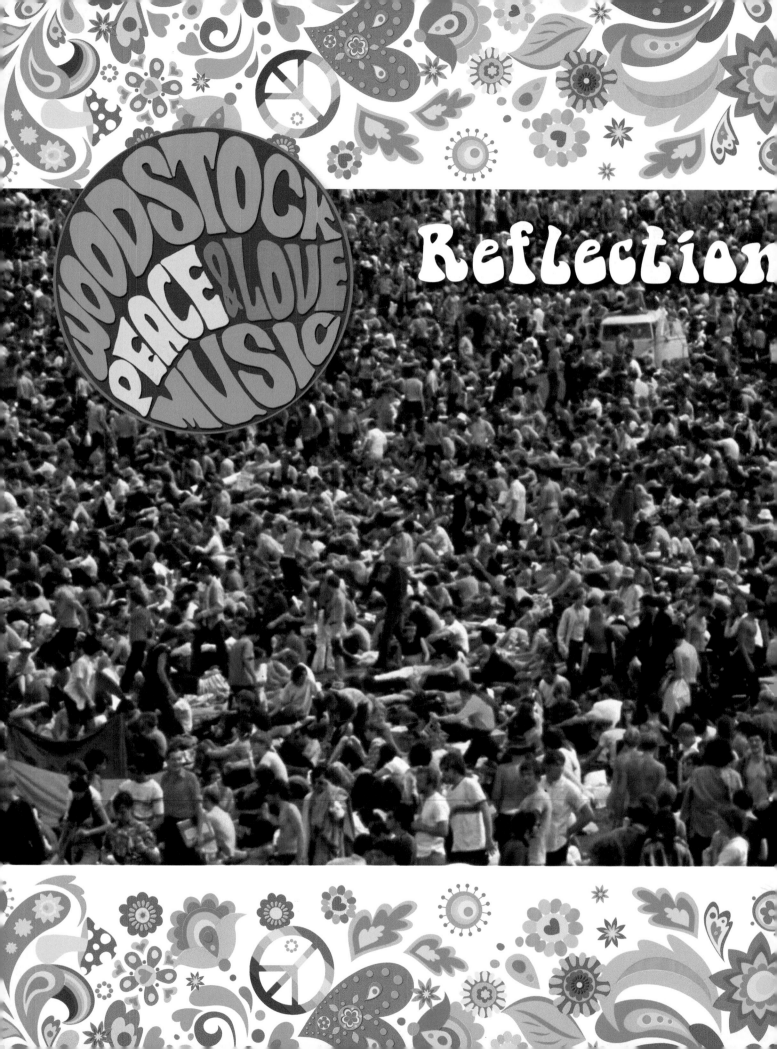

WOODSTOCK PEACE & LOVE MUSIC

Reflection